A'JA WILSON

Making a Difference as a WNBA Superstar

By Katie Kawa

I0807504

KidHaven PUBLISHING

People Who Make a Difference

Published in 2026 by
KidHaven Publishing, an Imprint of Greenhaven Publishing, LLC
2544 Clinton St.
Buffalo, NY 14224

Designer: Deanna Lepovich
Editor: Katie Kawa

Photo credits: Cover Xinhua/Alamy Stock Photo; p. 5 SPP Sport Press Photo./Alamy Stock Photo; pp. 7, 9, 20 Cal Sport Media/Alamy Stock Photo; p. 11 Zuma Press, Inc./Alamy Stock Photo; p. 13 UPI/Alamy Stock Photo; p. 15 Eyepix Group/Alamy Stock Photo; p. 17 Sipa USA/Alamy Stock Photo; p.19 Jennifer Graylock/Alamy Stock Photo; p. 21 T.Sumaetho/Shutterstock.com.

Cataloging-in-Publication Data

Names: Kawa, Katie.
Title: A'ja Wilson: making a difference as a WNBA superstar / Katie Kawa.
Description: Buffalo, NY : KidHaven Publishing, 2026. | Series: People who make a difference | Includes glossary and index.
Identifiers: ISBN 9781534549708 (pbk.) | ISBN 9781534549715 (library bound) | ISBN 9781534549722 (ebook)
Subjects: LCSH: Wilson, A'ja, 1996–Juvenile literature. | Women basketball players–United States–Biography–Juvenile literature. | African American women–United States–Biography–Juvenile literature.
Classification: LCC GV884.W67 K39 2026 | DDC 796.323092–dc23

Printed in the United States of America

Some of the images in this book illustrate individuals who are models. The depictions do not imply actual situations or events.

CPSIA compliance information: Batch #CSKH26: For further information contact Greenhaven Publishing LLC at 1-844-317-7404.

CONTENTS

MANY WAYS TO BE THE MVP

When a basketball player is named the MVP, it means they're the Most Valuable Player. This is an important title given to the player who makes the biggest difference on the court.

A'ja Wilson knows all about what it takes to be the MVP. She's been honored as the MVP of the Women's National Basketball Association (WNBA) and the Summer Olympics. However, A'ja is even more valuable off the court than she is on it. She's known for fighting for equality and helping young girls who look like her see themselves as valuable too.

In Her Words

"My goal is to not just ... be the best basketball player that I can be, but to also **inspire** the next **generation** that looks like me."

— "Voices for Change" interview with *People* magazine from July 2021

A'ja Wilson became a WNBA MVP while playing for the Las Vegas Aces. The WNBA is the top **professional** league, or group of teams, for women's basketball in the United States. A'ja has been one of the league's brightest stars for many years.

A BRIGHT SPOT

A'ja Riyadh Wilson was born on August 8, 1996. Some people might argue that she was born to play basketball, because her father played professionally in Europe. However, it took a while before A'ja chose basketball as her sport.

School wasn't always easy for A'ja. It was hard being one of the only Black girls in a school of mostly white students. In addition, she struggled with reading. A'ja has a condition called dyslexia that makes it hard for her to read. Basketball became a bright spot for her. In 2014, she won a state **championship** and was named Player of the Year.

In Her Words

"Basketball started to make a lot more sense to me than school ever did."

— "Brute Strength" post on *The Players' Tribune* website from March 2018

A'ja grew up in Hopkins, South Carolina. After she finished high school, she started college at the University of South Carolina, staying close to home.

SUCCESS WITH COACH STALEY

In 2014, A'ja began playing college basketball at the University of South Carolina. Her coach was Dawn Staley, who had her own successful **career** as a WNBA player before becoming a coach.

In 2017, A'ja helped lead her team to a college basketball championship. She was named the Most Outstanding Player, which is similar to being named the MVP. The next year was A'ja's final year in college. Although she didn't win another championship, she was named National Player of the Year. A'ja finished her career at the University of South Carolina as the school's leading scorer and the leader in blocked shots.

In Her Words

"Say what you want, do what you want, however you please. But at the end of the day ... [we're] going to make you remember who we are, and we're going to win."

— Interview with ESPN from October 2024

A'ja is shown here wearing number 22 for the University of South Carolina. She plays center, which means her job is to score, get rebounds, and block the other team's shots. Being tall is helpful for being a center, and A'ja is more than 6 feet (1.8 m) tall!

ROOKIE OF THE YEAR

A'ja's success in college caught the attention of the WNBA. She was drafted, or chosen, first overall in the 2018 WNBA Draft by the Las Vegas Aces.

In May 2018, A'ja played in her first WNBA game. She scored 14 points in her first game, and she finished her first season with 682 points. Her high-scoring first season helped earn her the title of Rookie of the Year. This honor is given to the player who has the best rookie, or first, season in a given year. However, the Aces missed the **playoffs** that year. A'ja wanted to make sure that never happened again.

In Her Words

"You are enough. No, no, no ... more than enough. As a matter of fact, *the best is yet to come*."

— "Dear Black Women" post on *The Players' Tribune* website from March 2021

A'ja is shown here during her first home game for the Aces in 2018. This was also the first home game for the Aces as a team! The team went by other names and played in other cities before coming to Las Vegas in 2018.

BECOMING A CHAMPION

A'ja was able to help the Aces reach the WNBA playoffs in 2019. The next year, she helped them get all the way to the WNBA Finals, or championship. Although they lost to the Seattle Storm that year, A'ja had some individual success. She was named the league's MVP for the first time. That same year, A'ja joined the WNBA's Social Justice Council—a group formed to **respond** to issues such as **racism**.

In 2022, A'ja was once again named the WNBA's MVP, and she helped her team reach new heights of success. The Aces won their first WNBA championship that year by beating the Connecticut Sun.

In Her Words

"Yes, you see me in a uniform. Yes, you can see the banners, the trophies [prizes] and the rings. But behind all that, I'm a human. I'm a young Black girl ... trying to navigate [understand] this world that's not the nicest."

— Interview with ABC News from February 2024

After the Aces won the WNBA championship, they met with Kamala Harris, who was the vice president of the United States at the time. A'ja and her teammates are shown here meeting with the vice president.

BREAKING RECORDS

A'ja and the Aces made their way back to the WNBA Finals in 2023. That year, they faced the New York Liberty, and they beat them to become back-to-back WNBA champions. A'ja averaged more than 20 points and 11 rebounds in the Finals, which helped earn her the title of Finals MVP.

In 2024, A'ja won her second Olympic gold medal with Team USA and was named the MVP of the women's Olympic basketball tournament, or series of games. That year, A'ja also broke the WNBA's single-season scoring record. She then became the first WNBA player to score over 1,000 points in a season!

In Her Words

"You're on this earth for a reason, you have a gift. Use it and share it with the world."

— "Voices for Change" interview with *People* magazine from July 2021

In 2024, A'ja, who can be seen here wearing number 22 for the Aces, was named the WNBA's MVP for the third time.

RAISING AWARENESS

A'ja has become one of the WNBA's most famous faces, and she has used that fame to bring awareness to important issues. One issue that means a lot to her is the way female **athletes** are treated. She has spoken out about the unfair things people say about female athletes and the inequality in pay between male and female athletes.

A'ja has also written about topics such as **mental** health, dyslexia, and racism. She even wrote a book, *Dear Black Girls*, which came out in February 2024. A'ja's writing has helped many people, especially Black girls and women, feel less alone and more **confident**.

In Her Words

"To all my Black girls out there ... You don't have to be a WNBA player ... or a celebrity [famous person] to have an impact on someone else."

— "Dear Black Girls" post on *The Players' Tribune* website from July 2020

A'ja is shown here with a group of students who have copies of *Dear Black Girls*. In her writing, A'ja has been open about her mental health to **encourage** others to take care of themselves. She has said she wants women and girls to know that it's OK to not always be OK.

INSPIRING GIRLS

A'ja's impact on the lives of young women goes far beyond her writing. In 2019, she and her parents started the A'ja Wilson Foundation, which has worked to support girls in many different ways.

The foundation provides money to help girls with dyslexia. A'ja has also hosted summits, or meetings, for girls to learn about managing their money, taking care of their mental health, and building confidence. Her work has made a big difference! In 2024, she was named the winner of the WNBA's Dawn Staley Community Leadership Award, which is a prize named after her college coach.

In Her Words

"At the end of the day, there are *different paths* to greatness. And I feel like we don't hear that message enough, especially as Black women."

— "Dear Black Women" post on *The Players' Tribune* website from March 2021

The Life of A'ja Wilson

1996
A'ja Wilson is born on August 8.

2014
A'ja's basketball team wins the high school state championship, she is named Player of the Year, and she begins college at the University of South Carolina.

2017
A'ja wins the national college basketball championship and is named the tournament's Most Outstanding Player.

2018
The Las Vegas Aces draft A'ja first overall, and she is named the WNBA's Rookie of the Year.

2019
A'ja and the Aces make the playoffs for the first time, and she starts the A'ja Wilson Foundation with her parents.

2020
A'ja joins the WNBA's Social Justice Council and is named the WNBA MVP.

2021
A'ja wins a gold medal at the Summer Olympics.

2022
The Aces win the WNBA championship, and A'ja is named WNBA MVP for a second time.

2023
The Aces win another championship, and A'ja is named MVP of the Finals.

2024
A'ja comes out with the book *Dear Black Girls*, wins another Olympic gold medal, sets the WNBA's single-season scoring record, and wins the MVP and Dawn Staley Community Leadership awards.

2025
A'ja is named one of *TIME* magazine's Women of the Year.

A'ja's life is full of high points, but she has also been open about the lows she had to work through to get to those high points. She has said that leaning on people she trusts during those low points helped her find her way again.

AN INFLUENTIAL ATHLETE

A'ja's success on the basketball court and her work to help others off of it have made her a very influential athlete. This is an athlete who has a lot of power to inspire others and make a difference. In fact, A'ja was named one of *TIME* magazine's 100 most influential people in the world for 2024.

TIME magazine honored A'ja again in 2025—this time naming her one of its Women of the Year. A'ja Wilson has created a space for herself in the spotlight, and she's using it to show just how skilled, strong, and supportive female athletes can be.

In Her Words

"I would say to that little girl with an apostrophe in her name: Don't let anyone stop you."

— "Voices for Change" interview with *People* magazine from July 2021

Be Like A'ja Wilson!

Raise money for groups that support people with dyslexia or conditions like it.

Learn more about racism, and listen respectfully to the stories of people who have dealt with it.

Take care of your mental health by doing activities that make you feel calm and happy, and encourage your friends and family to do the same.

Go with a trusted adult to a women's sporting event, or watch one on TV.

Pay attention to times when you or people around you use stereotypes—unfair and often untrue judgments about groups of people, such as female athletes or Black women. Work to avoid stereotypes in your own life, and help others avoid them too.

Be proud of your successes, and encourage people in your life to be proud of theirs.

If you are having a hard time in school or with your mental health, tell a trusted adult so you can get the help you need.

Write a letter to someone you know who needs support.

Tell a trusted adult if you see someone being treated unfairly or unkindly.

A'ja Wilson has inspired people to take care of themselves and those around them. These are just some ways you can do that in your own life!

GLOSSARY

athlete: A person who plays a sport.

career: A period of time spent doing a job or activity.

championship: A contest to find out who's the best player or team in a sport.

confident: Having a feeling of belief that you can do something well.

encourage: To make someone more likely to do something.

generation: A group of people born and living during the same time.

inspire: To move someone to do something great.

mental: Relating to the mind.

playoffs: A series of games played after the regular season of a sport is over to find out who the best team is that season.

professional: Having to do with a job someone does for a living.

racism: The practice of treating others poorly because they are part of a different race, or group of people who look alike in certain ways.

respond: To do something as a reaction to something that has happened.

FOR MORE INFORMATION

WEBSITES

A'ja Wilson Foundation

www.ajawilsonfoundation.org

Visit the official website of the A'ja Wilson Foundation to learn more about the work the foundation is doing and to see photos and videos of events the foundation has put together.

Full Bio: A'ja Wilson

aces.wnba.com/aja-wilson-bio

The official website of the Las Vegas Aces provides a helpful list of facts about A'ja's career.

BOOKS

Abell, Tracy. *A'ja Wilson*. Lake Elmo, MN: Focus Readers, 2022.

Hill, Anne E. *A'ja Wilson*. Minneapolis, MN: Lerner Publications, 2022.

Tischler, Joe. *A'ja Wilson*. Mankato, MN: Amicus Learning, 2025.

Publisher's note to educators and parents: Our editors have carefully reviewed these websites to ensure that they are suitable for students. Many websites change frequently, however, and we cannot guarantee that a site's future contents will continue to meet our high standards of quality and educational value. Be advised that students should be closely supervised whenever they access the internet.

INDEX